P9-BBS-704

To

_____

From

_____

Date

_____

50 Daily Devotions

for Kids only

Kindness

Copyright ©2008 Family Christian Stores

All rights reserved. No part of this book may be reproduced, stored in a retrieval system, or transmitted in any form or by any means—electronic, mechanical, photocopying, recording, or any other—except for brief quotations in printed reviews, without prior written permission of the publisher.
FAMILY CHRISTIAN STORES
Grand Rapids, MI 49530

The quoted ideas expressed in this book (but not scripture verses) are not, in all cases, exact quotations, as some have been edited for clarity and brevity. In all cases, the author has attempted to maintain the speaker's original intent. In some cases, quoted material for this book was obtained from secondary sources, primarily print media. While every effort was made to ensure the accuracy of these sources, the accuracy cannot be guaranteed. For additions, deletions, corrections or clarifications in future editions of this text, please write FAMILY CHRISTIAN STORES.

Scripture quotations are taken from:

The Holy Bible, New International Version (NIV) Copyright © 1973, 1978, 1984, by International Bible Society. Used by permission of Zondervan Publishing House. All rights reserved.

The Holy Bible, New King James Version (NKJV) Copyright © 1982 by Thomas Nelson, Inc. Used by permission.

Holy Bible, New Living Translation, (NLT) copyright © 1996. Used by permission of Tyndale House Publishers, Inc., Wheaton, Illinois 60189. All rights reserved.

The Message (MSG)- This edition issued by contractual arrangement with NavPress, a division of The Navigators, U.S.A. Originally published by NavPress in English as THE MESSAGE: The Bible in Contemporary Language copyright 2002-2003 by Eugene Peterson. All rights reserved.

New Century Version®. (NCV) Copyright © 1987, 1988, 1991 by Word Publishing, a division of Thomas Nelson, Inc. All rights reserved. Used by permission.

International Children's Bible®, New Century Version®. (ICB) Copyright © 1986, 1988, 1999 by Tommy Nelson™, a division of Thomas Nelson, Inc. All rights reserved. Used by permission.

The Holman Christian Standard Bible™ (HOLMAN CSB) Copyright © 1999, 2000, 2001 by Holman Bible Publishers. Used by permission.

Cover Design and Page Layout by Bart Dawson

ISBN 978-1-60587-003-8

Printed in the United States of America

50 Daily Devotions

for Kids only

Kindness

A Message to Parents

If your child's bookshelf is already spilling over with a happy assortment of good books for kids, congratulations—that means you're a thoughtful parent who understands the importance of reading to your child.

This little book is an important addition to your child's library. It is intended to be read by Christian parents to their young children. The text contains 50 brief chapters. Each chapter consists of a Bible verse, a brief story or lesson, kid-friendly quotations from notable Christian thinkers, a tip for kids, and a prayer. Every chapter examines a different aspect of an important Biblical theme: kindness.

For the next 50 days, take the time to read one chapter each night to your child, and then spend a few moments talking about the chapter's meaning. By the time you finish the book, you will have had 50 different opportunities to share God's wisdom with your son or daughter, and that's good . . . very good.

If you have been touched by God's love and His grace, then you know the joy that He has brought into your own life. Now it's your turn to share His message with the boy or girl whom He has entrusted to your care. Happy reading! And may God richly bless you and your family now and forever.

Day 1

Kindness Starts with You!

We must not become tired of doing good.
We will receive our harvest
of eternal life at the right time.
We must not give up!

Galatians 6:9 ICB

If you're waiting for other people to be nice to you before you're nice to them, you've got it backwards. Kindness starts with you! You see, you can never control what other people will say or do, but you can control your own behavior.

The Bible tells us that we should never stop doing good deeds as long as we live. Kindness is God's way, and it should be our way, too. Starting now!

When you launch an act of kindness out
into the crosswinds of life,
it will blow kindness back to you.

Dennis Swanberg

A Kid's Tip!

Kindness every day: Kindness should be part of our
lives every day, not just on the days when we feel
good. Don't try to be kind some of the time, and
don't try to be kind to some of the people you know.
Instead, try to be kind all of the time, and try to
be kind to all the people you know. Remember, the
Golden Rule starts with you!

A Parent's Tip!

Kindness matters: When you make the decision to
be a genuinely kind person, you'll make decisions that
improve your own life and the lives of your family
and friends.

Today's Prayer

Dear Lord, help me to remember
that it is always my job to treat
others with kindness and respect.
Make the Golden Rule my rule and make
Your Word my guidebook for
the way I treat other people.
Amen

Day 2

The Rule That's Golden

Do for other people the same things
you want them to do for you.

Matthew 7:12 ICB

Some rules are easier to understand than they are to live by. Jesus told us that we should treat other people in the same way that we would want to be treated: that's the Golden Rule. But sometimes, especially when we're tired or upset, that rule is very hard to follow.

Jesus wants us to treat other people with respect, love, kindness, and courtesy. When we do, we make our families and friends happy . . . and we make our Father in heaven very proud. So if you're wondering how to treat someone else, ask the person you see every time you look into the mirror. The answer you receive will tell you exactly what to do.

When you extend hospitality to others,
you're not trying to impress people,
you're trying to reflect God to them.

Max Lucado

A Kid's Tip!

How would you feel? When you're trying to decide
how to treat another person, ask yourself this
question: "How would I feel if somebody treated me
that way?" Then, treat the other person the way
that you would want to be treated.

A Parent's Tip!

The Golden Rule . . . is as good as gold—in fact, it's
better than gold. And as a responsible parent, you
should make certain that your child knows that the
Golden Rule is, indeed, golden.

Today's Prayer

Dear Lord, help me always to do my very best to treat others as I wish to be treated. The Golden Rule is Your rule, Father; let me also make it mine.
Amen

Day 3

Kind Words

When you talk, do not say
harmful things. But say what people
need—words that will help them become
stronger. Then what you say will help
those who listen to you.

Ephesians 4:29 ICB

Do you like for people to say kind words to you? Of course you do! And that's exactly how other people feel, too. That's why it's so important to say things that make people feel better, not worse.

Your words can help people . . . or not. Make certain that you're the kind of person who says helpful things, not hurtful things. And, make sure that you're the kind of person who helps other people feel better about themselves, not worse.

Everybody needs to hear kind words, and that's exactly the kind of words they should hear from you!

We will always experience regret when we live
for the moment and do not weigh our words
and deeds before we give them life.

Lisa Bevere

A Kid's Tip!

If you can't think of something nice to say . . . don't
say anything. It's better to say nothing than to hurt
someone's feelings.

A Parent's Tip!

Parents set the boundaries: Whether they realize it
or not, parents (not kids) establish the general tone
of the conversations that occur within their homes.
And it's up to parents to ensure that the tone of
those conversations is a tone that's pleasing to God.

Today's Prayer

Dear Lord, You hear every word
that I say. Help me remember
to speak words that are honest,
kind, and helpful.
Amen

Day 4

How Would Jesus Behave?

Love other people just as
Christ loved us.

Ephesians 5:2 ICB

If you're not sure whether something is right or wrong—kind or unkind—ask yourself a simple question: "How would Jesus behave if He were here?" The answer to that question will tell you what to do.

Jesus was perfect, but we are not. Still, we must try as hard as we can to do the best that we can. When we do, we will love others, just as Christ loves us.

The only source of Life is the Lord Jesus Christ.

Oswald Chambers

A Kid's Tip!

Learning about Jesus: Start learning about Jesus, and keep learning about Him as long as you live. His story never grows old, and His teachings never fail.

A Parent's Tip!

Try as we might, we simply cannot escape the consequences of our actions. How we behave today has a direct impact on the rewards we will receive tomorrow. That's a lesson that we must teach our children by our words and our actions, but not necessarily in that order.

Today's Prayer

Dear Lord, let me use Jesus as my guide
for living. When I have questions about
what to do or how to act, let me behave
as He behaved. When I do, I will share
His love with my family, with my friends,
and with the world.

Amen

Day 5

Do Yourself a Favor

A kind person is doing himself a favor.
But a cruel person brings trouble
upon himself.

Proverbs 11:17 ICB

King Solomon wrote most of the Book of Proverbs; in it, he gave us wonderful advice for living wisely. Solomon warned that unkind behavior leads only to trouble, but kindness is its own reward.

The next time you're tempted to say an unkind word, remember Solomon. He was one of the wisest men who ever lived, and he knew that it's always better to be kind. And now, you know it, too.

Change the heart, and you change the speech.

Warren Wiersbe

A Kid's Tip!

Sorry you said it? Apologize! Did you say something that hurt someone's feelings? Then it's time for an apology: yours. It's never too late to apologize, but it's never too early, either!

A Parent's Tip!

Don't be afraid to preach sermons . . . Occasionally. Don't be afraid to talk with your child about your core beliefs, and never be afraid to discuss matters of personal safety or health. But, don't make your sermons too frequent or too condescending.

Today's Prayer

Dear Lord, let me be a kind person.
Let me be quick to share and quick to
forgive. And when I make mistakes,
let me be quick to change
and quick to ask forgiveness
from others and from You.
Amen

Day 6

The Good Samaritan

Help each other with your troubles.
When you do this, you truly obey
the law of Christ.

Galatians 6:2 ICB

Jesus told the story of a Jewish man who had been attacked by robbers. Luckily, a kind Samaritan happened by. And even though Jews and Samaritans were enemies, the Samaritan rescued the injured man.

And the meaning of the story is this: Jesus wants us to be kind to everyone, not just to our families and our friends. Jesus wants us to be good neighbors to all people, not just to those who are exactly like us.

Are you a good Samaritan? If so, you're doing the right thing, and that's exactly how God wants you to behave.

How busy we have become . . .
and as a result, how empty!

Charles Swindoll

A Kid's Tip!

Look around: Someone very near you may need a
helping hand or a kind word, so keep your eyes open,
and look for people who need your help, whether at
home, at church, or at school.

A Parent's Tip!

When it comes to teaching our children about
helping others, our sermons are not as important as
our service. Be sure you show your kids, not just tell
them, what it means to be a good samaritan.

Today's Prayer

Dear Lord, make me a Good Samaritan.
Let me never be too busy or too proud
to help a person in need. You have given
me so many blessings, Lord. Let me share
those blessings with others today
and every day that I live.
Amen

Day 7

When People Are Not Nice

If someone does wrong to you,
do not pay him back by
doing wrong to him.

Romans 12:17 ICB

Sometimes people aren't nice, and that's when we feel like striking back in anger. But the Bible tells us not to do it. As Christians, we should not repay one bad deed with another bad deed. Instead, we should forgive the other person as quickly as we can.

Are you angry at someone? If so, then it's time to forgive him or her. Jesus does not intend that your heart be troubled by anger. Your heart should instead be filled with love, just as Jesus' heart was . . . and is!

We are all fallen creatures
and all very hard to live with.

C. S. Lewis

A Kid's Tip!

Forgive . . . and keep forgiving! Sometimes, you may forgive someone once and then, at a later time, become angry at the very same person again. If so, you must forgive that person again and again . . . until it sticks!

A Parent's Tip!

If it were easy, everybody would be doing it: Face facts: forgiveness can be a very hard thing to do. No matter. God instructs us to forgive others (and to keep forgiving them), period. As a parent, you must explain to your child that forgiving another person—even when it's difficult—is the right thing to do.

Today's Prayer

Dear Lord, whenever I am angry,
give me a forgiving heart. And help me
remember that the best day
to forgive somebody is this one.
Amen

Day 8

Pray About It!

Do not worry about anything.
But pray and ask God for
everything you need.

Philippians 4:6 ICB

If you are upset, pray about it. If you're having trouble being kind to someone, pray about it. If there is a person you don't like, pray for a forgiving heart. If there is something you're worried about, ask God to comfort you. And as you pray more, you'll discover that God is always near and that He's always ready to hear from you. So don't worry about things; pray about them. God is waiting . . . and listening!

God is always listening.

Stormie Omartian

A Kid's Tip!

Open-eyed prayers: When you are praying, your eyes don't always have to be closed. Of course it's good to close your eyes and bow your head, but you can also offer a quick prayer to God with your eyes open. That means that you can pray anytime you want.

A Parent's Tip!

Pray early and often. God is listening, and your children are watching.

Today's Prayer

Dear Lord, You are always near;
let me talk with You often. Let me use
prayer to find Your answers for my life
today and every day that I live.
Amen

Day 9

Being Honest and Kind

Good people will be guided by honesty.

Proverbs 11:3 ICB

Maybe you've heard this phrase: "Honesty is the best policy." But, honesty is not just the best policy; it is also God's policy.

An important part of becoming a good person is learning to tell the truth. Lies usually have a way of hurting people, so even when it's hard, we must be honest with others.

If we are going to follow the rules that God has given us, we must remember that truth is not just the best way; it is also His way. So be honest and kind . . . now!

God doesn't expect you to be perfect,
but he does insist on complete honesty.

Rick Warren

A Kid's Tip!

Honesty in action: Thinking about being an honest person isn't enough. If you want to be considered an honest person, you must tell the truth today and every day.

A Parent's Tip!

Discuss the importance of honesty. Teach the importance of honesty every day, and, if necessary, use words.

Today's Prayer

Dear Lord, sometimes it's hard to tell the truth. But even when telling the truth is difficult, let me follow Your commandment. Honesty isn't just the best policy, Lord; it's Your policy, and I will obey You by making it my policy, too.

Amen

Day 10

Making Friends

A friend loves you all the time.

Proverbs 17:17 ICB

The Bible tells us that friendship can be a wonderful thing. That's why it's good to know how to make and to keep good friends.

If you want to make lots of friends, practice the Golden Rule with everybody you know. Be kind, share, and say nice things. Be helpful. When you do, you'll discover that the Golden Rule isn't just a nice way to behave; it's also a great way to make and to keep friends!

The best times in life are made a thousand times better when shared with a dear friend.

Luci Swindoll

A Kid's Tip!

First, become interested in them . . . and soon they'll become interested in you!

A Parent's Tip!

Help from the sidelines: As parents, we can't make friendships for our children, but we can coach them on the art of making friends. All of us, whether youngsters or grown-ups, make friends by treating others as we wish to be treated. And if that sounds suspiciously like the Golden Rule, that's because it is the Golden Rule.

Today's Prayer

Dear Lord, help me to be a good friend.
Let me treat other people as I want to
be treated. Let me share my things,
and let me share kind words with
my friends and family,
today and every day.
Amen

Day 11

Sharing Your Stuff

God loves the person who
gives cheerfully.

2 Corinthians 9:7 NLT

How many times have you heard someone say, "Don't touch that; it's mine!" If you're like most of us, you've heard those words many times and you may have even said them yourself.

The Bible tells us that it's better for us to share things than it is to keep them all to ourselves. And the Bible also tells us that when we share, it's best to do so cheerfully. So today and every day, let's share. It's the best way because it's God's way.

He climbs highest who helps another up.

Zig Ziglar

A Kid's Tip!

Too many toys? Give them away! Are you one of those lucky kids who has more toys than you can play with? If so, remember that not everyone is so lucky. Ask your parents to help you give some of your toys to children who need them more than you do.

A Parent's Tip!

Good Samaritan 101: You're the teacher. Class is in session. Your child is in attendance. Actions speak louder than words. And it's one of the most important courses you will ever teach.

Today's Prayer

Dear Lord, You have given me so much.
Let me share my gifts with others,
and let me be a joyful and generous
Christian, today and every day.
Amen

Day 12

Making Other People Feel Better!

Let us think about each other
and help each other to show love
and do good deeds.

Hebrews 10:24 ICB

When other people are sad, what can we do? We can do our best to cheer them up by showing kindness and love.

The Bible tells us that we must care for each other, and when everybody is happy, that's an easy thing to do. But, when people are sad, for whatever reason, it's up to us to speak a kind word or to offer a helping hand.

Do you know someone who is discouraged or sad? If so, perhaps it's time to take matters into your own hands. Think of something you can do to cheer that person up . . . and then do it! You'll make two people happy.

Encouraging others means helping people,
looking for the best in them, and trying to
bring out their positive qualities.

John Maxwell

A Kid's Tip!

Cheering someone up without saying a word: If
you want to cheer someone up but can't think of
something to say or do, try drawing a picture or
writing a note.

A Parent's Tip!

Goodness is as goodness does: In order to be a good
person, you must do good things. Thinking about
them isn't enough. So get busy! Your family and
friends need all the good deeds they can get!

Today's Prayer

Dear Lord, make me a loving, encouraging Christian. And, let my love for Jesus be reflected through the kindness that I show to those who need the healing touch of the Master's hand.

Amen

Day 13

Being Kind to Parents

Honor your father and your mother.

Exodus 20:12 ICB

We love our parents so very much, but sometimes, we may take them for granted. When we take them "for granted," that means that we don't give them the honor and respect they deserve.

The Bible tells us to honor our parents. That's God's rule, and it's also the best way to live. When we treat our parents with the respect they deserve, we show them that we appreciate all they have done for us. And that's so much better than taking our parents for granted, and if you don't believe it, just ask them!

What lessons about honor did you learn
from your childhood?
Are you living what you learned today?

Dennis Swanberg

A Kid's Tip!

Two magic words: Thank you! Your parents will never
become tired of hearing those two little words. And
while you're at it, try three more: "I love you!"

A Parent's Tip!

Two magic words: Thank you! Your kids learn from
your action and your words. And while you're at it,
don't forget these three: "I love you!"

Today's Prayer

Dear Lord, make me respectful
and thankful. Let me give honor
and love to my parents,
and let my behavior be pleasing
to them . . . and to You.
Amen

Day 14

Cheerfulness Now

A happy heart is like
a continual feast.

Proverbs 15:15 NCV

What is a continual feast? It's a little bit like a non-stop birthday party: fun, fun, and more fun! The Bible tells us that a cheerful heart can make life like a continual feast, and that's something worth working for.

Where does cheerfulness begin? It begins inside each of us; it begins in the heart. So today and every day, let's be thankful to God for His blessings, and let's show our thanks by sharing good cheer wherever we go. This old world needs all the cheering up it can get . . . and so do we!

When we bring sunshine into the lives of others,
we're warmed by it ourselves.
When we spill a little happiness, it splashes on us.

Barbara Johnson

A Kid's Tip!

Cheer up somebody else. Do you need a little cheering up? If so, find somebody else who needs cheering up, too. Then, do your best to brighten that person's day. When you do, you'll discover that cheering up other people is a wonderful way to cheer yourself up, too.

A Parent's Tip!

Cheerfulness is contagious: Remember that a cheerful family starts with cheerful parents.

Today's Prayer

Dear Lord, make me a cheerful Christian.
Today, let me celebrate my blessings
and my life; let me be quick to smile
and slow to become angry.
And, let Your love shine in me
and through me.
Amen

Who deserves our respect? Grown-ups? Of course. Teachers? Certainly. Family members? Yes. Friends? That's right, but it doesn't stop there. The Bible teaches us to treat all people with respect.

Respect for others is habit-forming: the more we do it, the easier it becomes. So start practicing right now. Say lots of kind words and do lots of kind things, because when it comes to kindness and respect, practice makes perfect.

Day 15

Be Kind to Everyone

Show respect for all people.
Love the brothers and sisters
of God's family.

1 Peter 2:17 ICB

Be so preoccupied with good will
that you haven't room for ill will.

E. Stanley Jones

A Kid's Tip!

Respecting all kinds of people: Make sure that you show proper respect for everyone, even if that person happens to be different from you. It's easy to make fun of people who seem different . . . but it's wrong.

A Parent's Tip!

Respect for authority starts with you. Remember this: respect for those in authority begins at the head of the household and works its way down from there. And remember one more thing: your kids are watching every move you make!

Today's Prayer

Dear Lord, help me to be kind to
everyone I meet. Help me to be
respectful to all people,
not just teachers and parents.
Help me to say kind words and do
good deeds, today and every day.
Amen

Day 16

Say a Kind Word

The right word spoken at the right time
is as beautiful as gold apples
in a silver bowl.

Proverbs 25:11 ICB

How hard is it to speak with kind words? Not very! Yet sometimes we're so busy that we forget to say the very things that might make other people feel better.

We should always try to say nice things to our families and friends. And when we feel like saying something that's not so nice, perhaps we should stop and think before we say it. Kind words help; cruel words hurt. It's as simple as that. And, when we say the right thing at the right time, we give a gift that can change someone's day or someone's life.

How many people stop because so few say, "Go!"

Charles Swindoll

A Kid's Tip!

If you don't know what to say . . . don't say anything. Sometimes, a hug works better than a whole mouthful of words.

A Parent's Tip!

Words matter: The words you speak will help shape the kids you love . . . and once you speak those words, you cannot "un-speak" them. Even if you're not speaking directly to your kids, you can be sure that your kids are listening, so choose your words carefully.

Today's Prayer

Dear Lord, help me to say the right thing
at the right time. Let me choose
my words carefully so that I can help
other people and glorify You.
Amen

Day 17

God Knows the Heart

I am the Lord, and I can look
into a person's heart.

Jeremiah 17:10 ICB

You can try to keep secrets from other people, but you can't keep secrets from God. God knows what you think and what you do. And, if you want to please God, you must start with good intentions and a kind heart.

If your heart tells you not to do something, don't do it! If your conscience tells you that something is wrong, stop! If you feel ashamed by something you've done, don't do it ever again! You can keep secrets from other people some of the time, but God is watching all of the time, and He sees everything, including your heart.

Our actions are seen by people,
but our motives are monitored by God.

Franklin Graham

A Kid's Tip!

That little voice inside your head . . . is called your conscience. Listen to it; it's usually right!

A Parent's Tip!

Your kids are watching: If you're overly concerned with "keeping up appearances," your child will be too. So, whenever you're faced with the choice of pleasing your neighbors or pleasing God, make the right choice. If you concentrate on pleasing God, your child will learn what's important . . . and what's not.

Today's Prayer

Dear Lord, other people see me from
the outside, but You know my heart.
Let my heart be pure, and let me listen
to the voice that You have placed there,
today and always.

Amen

Day 18

Be Gentle

Pleasant words are like a honeycomb.
They make a person happy and healthy.

Proverbs 16:24 ICB

The Bible says that using gentle words is helpful and that using cruel words is not. But sometimes, especially when we're frustrated or angry, our words and our actions may not be so gentle. Sometimes, we may say things or do things that are unkind or hurtful to others. When we do, we're wrong.

So the next time you're tempted to strike out in anger, don't. And if you want to help your family and friends, remember that gentle words are better than harsh words and good deeds are better than the other kind. Always!

How delightful a teacher,
but gentle a provider, how bountiful
a giver is my Father! Praise, praise to Thee,
O manifested Most High.

Jim Elliot

A Kid's Tip!

Gentle is as gentle does: In order to be a gentle person, you must do gentle things. Thinking about them isn't enough. So get busy! Your family and friends need all the gentleness they can get!

A Parent's Tip!

Gentleness is contagious; kids can catch it from their parents.

Today's Prayer

Dear Lord, help me to keep away
from angry thoughts and angry people.
And if I am tempted to have
a temper tantrum, help me
to calm down before I do.
Amen

Day 19

Telling Tales

A person who gossips ruins friendships.

Proverbs 16:28 ICB

Do you know what gossip is? It's when we say bad things about people who are not around. When we gossip, we hurt others and we hurt ourselves. That's why the Bible tells us that gossip is wrong.

Sometimes, it's tempting to say bad things about people, and when we do, it makes us feel important . . . for a while. But, after a while, the bad things that we say come back to hurt us, and, of course, they hurt other people, too.

So if you want to be a kind person and a good friend, don't gossip . . . and don't listen to people who do.

Honesty has a beautiful and refreshing simplicity
about it. No ulterior motives. No hidden meanings.
As honesty and integrity characterize our lives,
there will be no need to manipulate others.

Charles Swindoll

A Kid's Tip!

Watch what you say: Don't say something behind
someone's back that you wouldn't say to that person
directly.

A Parent's Tip!

Honesty at school starts at home. Don't expect
teachers to teach the lessons that parents should
have already taught!

Today's Prayer

Dear Lord, I know that I have influence
on many people . . . make me a good
influence. And let the words that
I speak today be worthy of the One
who has saved me forever.
Amen

Day 20

Paul and His Friends

I thank my God every time
I remember you.

Philippians 1:3 NIV

In his letter to the Philippians, Paul wrote to his distant friends saying that he thanked God every time He remembered them. We, too, should thank God for the family and friends He has brought into our lives.

Today, let's give thanks to God for all the people who love us, for brothers and sisters, parents and grandparents, aunts and uncles, cousins, and friends. And then, as a way of thanking God, let's obey Him by being especially kind to our loved ones. They deserve it, and so does He.

Thanksgiving is good but Thanksliving is better.

Jim Gallery

A Kid's Tip!

The mailman can help: If you have friends or relatives who are far away, send them letters or drawings (your mom or dad will be happy to mail them for you). Everybody loves to receive mail, and so will your family members and friends.

A Parent's Tip!

Think about His blessings: Today, as you hug your child or kiss your spouse—or as you gaze upon a passing cloud or marvel at a glorious sunset—think of what God has done for you and yours. And, every time you notice a gift from the Giver of all things good, praise Him. His works are marvelous, His gifts are beyond understanding, and His love endures forever.

Today's Prayer

Dear Lord, thank You for my family and
my friends. Let me show kindness to
all of them: those who are here at home
and those who are far away.
Then, my family and friends will know
that I remember them and love them,
today and every day.
Amen

Day 21

When You're Angry

A foolish person loses his temper.
But a wise person controls his anger.

Proverbs 29:11 ICB

When you're angry, you will be tempted to say things and do things that you'll regret later. So don't do them! Instead of doing things in a hurry, slow down long enough to calm yourself down.

Jesus does not intend that you strike out against other people, and He doesn't intend that your heart be troubled by anger. Your heart should instead be filled with love, just like Jesus' heart was . . . and is!

Bitterness and anger,
usually over trivial things, make havoc of homes,
churches, and friendships.

Warren Wiersbe

A Kid's Tip!

Think carefully . . . make that very carefully! If
you're a little angry, think carefully before you
speak. If you're very angry, think very carefully.
Otherwise, you might say something in anger that
you'll regret later.

A Parent's Tip!

Wise role models are a good thing to have: If you
can control your anger, you'll help your children see
the wisdom in controlling theirs.

Today's Prayer

Dear Lord, I can be so impatient, and I can become so angry. Calm me down, Lord, and make me a patient, forgiving Christian. Just as You have forgiven me, let me forgive others so that I can follow the example of Your Son.

Amen

When People Can't Help Themselves

I tell you the truth, whatever you did
for one of the least of these
brothers of mine, you did for me.

Matthew 25:40 NIV

Perhaps you have lots of advantages. Some people don't. Perhaps you have the benefit of a loving family, a strong faith in God, and three good meals each day. Some people don't. Perhaps you were lucky enough to be born into a country where people are free. Some people weren't.

Jesus instructed us to care for those who can't care for themselves, wherever they may be. And, when we do something nice for someone in need, we have also done a good deed for our Savior. So today, look for someone who needs your help, and then do your best to help him or her. God is watching and waiting. The next move is yours.

People don't care how much you know
until they know how much you care.

John Maxwell

A Kid's Tip!

When am I old enough to start giving? If you're
old enough to understand these words, you're old
enough to start giving to your church and to those
who are less fortunate than you. If you're not sure
about the best way to do it, ask your parents!

A Parent's Tip!

Preach, teach, and reach . . . out!: Charity should
start at home—with parents—and work its way down
the family tree from there.

Today's Prayer

Dear Lord, You have given me so many blessings. Make me a cheerful, generous giver, Lord, as I share the blessings that You first shared with me.

Amen

Do you want to be happy? Here are some things you should do: Love God and His Son, Jesus; obey the Golden Rule; and always try to do the right thing. When you do these things, you'll discover that happiness goes hand-in-hand with good behavior.

The happiest people do not misbehave; the happiest people are not cruel or greedy. The happiest people don't say unkind things. The happiest people are those who love God and follow his rules—starting, of course, with the Golden one.

Day 23

How to Be Happy

Those who want to do right more than anything else are happy.

Matthew 5:6 ICB

Learning how to forgive and forget is one
of the secrets of a happy Christian life.

Warren Wiersbe

A Kid's Tip!

Sometimes happy, sometimes not: Even if you're a
very good person, you shouldn't expect to be happy
all the time. Sometimes, things will happen to make
you sad, and it's okay to be sad when bad things
happen to you or to your friends and family. But
remember: through good times and bad, you'll always
be happier if you obey the rules of your Father in
heaven. So obey them!

A Parent's Tip!

Happiness at home: Your children deserve to grow
up in a happy home . . . and you owe to them (and to
yourself) to provide that kind of home.

Today's Prayer

Dear Lord, make me the kind of Christian who earns happiness by doing the right thing. When I obey Your rules, Father, I will find the joy that You have in store for me. Let me find Your joy, Lord, today and always.

Amen

Day 24

What James Said

This royal law is found in the Scriptures:
"Love your neighbor as yourself."
If you obey this law,
then you are doing right.

James 2:8 ICB

James was the brother of Jesus and a leader of the early Christian church. In a letter that is now a part of the New Testament, James reminded his friends of a "royal law." That law is the Golden Rule.

When we treat others in the same way that we wish to be treated, we are doing the right thing. James knew it and so, of course, did his brother Jesus. Now we should learn the same lesson: it's nice to be nice; it's good to be good; and it's great to be kind.

Inasmuch as love grows in you, so beauty grows.
For love is the beauty of the soul.

St. Augustine

A Kid's Tip!

Kind is as kind does: In order to be a kind person, you must do kind things. Thinking about them isn't enough. So get busy! Your family and friends need all the kindness they can get!

A Parent's Tip!

When in doubt, be a little kinder than necessary. Your children are making mental notes.

Today's Prayer

Dear Lord, it's easy to be kind to some
people and difficult to be kind to others.
Let me be kind to all people so that
I might follow in the footsteps
of Your Son.
Amen

Day 25

Doing What's Right

Doing what is right brings freedom
to honest people.

Proverbs 11:6 ICB

Sometimes, it's so much easier to do the wrong thing than it is to do the right thing, especially when we're tired or frustrated. But, doing the wrong thing almost always leads to trouble. And sometimes, it leads to BIG trouble.

When you do the right thing, you don't have to worry about what you did or what you said. But, when you do the wrong thing, you'll be worried that someone will find out. So do the right thing, which, by the way, also happens to be the kind thing. You'll be glad you did, and so will other people!

There may be no trumpet sound or loud applause
when we make a right decision,
just a calm sense of resolution and peace.

Gloria Gaither

A Kid's Tip!

Think ahead: Before you do something, ask yourself this question: "Will I be ashamed if my parents find out?" If the answer to that question is "Yes," don't do it!

A Parent's Tip!

Think ahead: Before you do something, ask yourself this question: "Will I be ashamed if my kids find out?" Think before you do.

Today's Prayer

Dear Lord, I want to be a person who respects others, and I want to be a person who is kind. Wherever I am and whatever I do, let me be like Jesus in the way that I treat others, because with Him as my guide, I will do the right thing, today and forever.
Amen

Day 26

Love Your Enemies

I tell you, love your enemies.
Pray for those who hurt you.
If you do this, you will be true sons
of your Father in heaven.

Matthew 6:44-45 ICB

It's easy to love people who have been nice to you, but it's very hard to love people who have treated you badly. Still, Jesus instructs us to treat both our friends and our enemies with kindness and respect.

Are you having problems being nice to someone? Is there someone you know whom you don't like very much? Remember that Jesus not only forgave His enemies, He also loved them . . . and so should you.

Forgiveness is the precondition of love.

Catherine Marshall

A Kid's Tip!

Making up may not be as hard as you think! If there is someone who has been mean to you, perhaps it's time for the two of you to make up. If you're willing to be the first person to offer a kind word, you'll discover that making up is usually easier than you think.

A Parent's Tip!

Bearing a grudge = bearing a burden. You know what a heavy burden it can be to bear a grudge against another person; make sure that your child knows, too!

Today's Prayer

Dear Lord, give me a forgiving heart.
When I have bad feelings toward
another person, help me to forgive
them and to love them,
just as You forgive and love me.
Amen

His Name Was Barnabas

Barnabas was a good man,
full of the Holy Spirit and full of faith.

Acts 11:23-24 ICB

Barnabas was a leader in the early Christian church who was known for his kindness and for his ability to encourage others. Because of Barnabas, many people were introduced to Christ.

We become like Barnabas when we speak kind words to our families and to our friends. And then, because we have been generous and kind, the people around us can see how Christians should behave. So when in doubt, be kind and generous to others, just like Barnabas.

Do you wonder where you can go for
encouragement and motivation?
Run to Jesus.

Max Lucado

A Kid's Tip!

Be an encourager! Barnabas was known as a man who
encouraged others. In other words, he made other
people feel better by saying kind things. You, like
Barnabas, can encourage your family and friends . . .
and you should.

A Parent's Tip!

You know that your child is a unique gift from God
. . . make sure that your child hears that message
every day . . . from you.

Today's Prayer

Dear Lord, let me help to encourage
other people by the words that
I say and the things that I do. Let me be
a person who is always helpful
and kind to my friends and family.
And let them see Your love for me
reflected in my love for them.
Amen

Day 28

Don't Be Cruel!

Don't ever stop being kind and truthful.
Let kindness and truth show in all you do.

Proverbs 3:3 ICB

Sometimes, young people can be very mean. They can make fun of other people, and when they do so, it's wrong. Period.

As Christians, we should be kind to everyone. And, if other kids say unkind things to a child or make fun of him or her, it's up to us to step in, like the Good Samaritan, and lend a helping hand.

Today and every day, be a person who is known for your kindness, not for your cruelty. That's how God wants you to behave. Period.

Encouragement is the oxygen of the soul.

John Maxwell

A Kid's Tip!

Stand up and be counted! Do you know children who say or do cruel things to other kids? If so, don't join in! Instead, stand up for those who need your help. It's the right thing to do.

A Parent's Tip!

Parents make the best encouragers! You're not just your children's parents; you're their biggest fans. Make sure they know it.

Today's Prayer

Dear Lord, when I see meanness in this
world, let me do my best to correct it.
When I see people who are hurting,
let me do my best to help them.
And when I am hurt by others,
let me do my best to forgive them.
Amen

Day 29

The Things We Say

A good person's words
will help many others.

Proverbs 10:21 ICB

The words that we speak are very important because of how they effect other people. The things that we say can either help people or hurt them. We can either make people feel better, or we can hurt their feelings.

The Bible reminds us that words are powerful things; we must use them carefully. Let's use our words to help our families and friends. When we do, we make their lives better and our own.

Attitude and the spirit in which we communicate
are as important as the words we say.

Charles Stanley

A Kid's Tip!

Think first, speak second: If you want to keep from
hurting other people's feelings, don't open your
mouth until you've turned on your brain.

A Parent's Tip!

Parental Encouragement 101: Encouragement is
an essential ingredient in healthy parent-child
communications. Make sure that you encourage your
child by communicating your love, your admiration,
and your devotion—and make certain that you do so
many times each day.

Today's Prayer

Dear Lord, make my words pleasing
to You. Let the words that I say
and the things that I do help others
to feel better about themselves
and to know more about You.
Amen

Day 30

It Starts in the Heart

Blessed are the pure of heart,
for they will see God.

Matthew 5:8 NIV

Where does kindness start? It starts in our hearts and works its way out from there. Jesus taught us that a pure heart is a wonderful blessing. It's up to each of us to fill our hearts with love for God, love for Jesus, and love for all people. When we do, we are blessed.

Do you want to be the best person you can be? Then invite the love of Christ into your heart and share His love with your family and friends. And remember that lasting love always comes from a pure heart . . . like yours!

The mind is a faculty,
and magnificent one at that.
But the heart is the dwelling place
of our true beliefs.

John Eldredge

A Parent's Tip and a Kid's Tip!

Learn about Jesus and His attitude. Then try and do what Jesus would do.

Today's Prayer

Dear Lord, give me a heart that is pure.
Let me live by Your Word
and trust in Your Son today and forever.
Amen

Day 31

Don't Lose Your Temper

And be careful that when you get
on each other's nerves you don't snap
at each other. Look for the best
in each other, and always do
your best to bring it out.

1 Thessalonians 5:15 MSG

Temper tantrums are so silly. And so is pouting. So, of course, is whining. When we lose our tempers, we say things that we shouldn't say, and we do things that we shouldn't do. Too bad!

The Bible tells us that it is foolish to become angry and that it is wise to remain calm. That's why we should learn to control our tempers before our tempers control us.

When you lose your temper . . . you lose.

Jim Gallery

A Kid's Tip!

No more temper tantrums! If you think you're about to throw a tantrum, slow down, catch your breath, and walk away if you must. It's better to walk away than it is to strike out in anger.

A Parent's Tip!

Time out ain't just for your kids!: Have you ever had to send your kid to "time out"? Well you need to be ready to send yourself there, too. If you become angry, the time to step away from the situation is before you say unkind words or do unkind things— not after. So it's perfectly okay to place yourself in "time out" until you can calm down.

Today's Prayer

Lord, when I become angry, help me to
remember that You offer me peace.
Let me turn to You for wisdom,
for patience, and for the peace
that only You can give.
Amen

Day 32

Don't Worry

Give all your worries and cares to God,
for he cares about what happens to you.

1 Peter 5:6 NLT

If you're feeling upset, what should you do? Well, you should talk to your parents and there's something else you can do: you can pray about it.

If there is person you don't like, you should pray for a forgiving heart. If there is something you're worried about, you should ask God to give you comfort. And as you pray more, you'll discover that God is always near and that He's always ready to hear from you. So don't worry about things; pray about them. God is waiting patiently to hear from you . . . and He's ready to listen NOW!

The more you meditate on God's Word,
the less you will have to worry about.

Rick Warren

A Kid's Tip!

If you're worried about something, talk to your parents and pray to God. When you do these things, you'll feel better in a hurry.

A Parent's Tip!

Categorize your worries: Carefully divide your areas of concern into two categories: those things you can control and those you cannot control. Once you've done so, spend your time working to resolve the things you can control, and entrust everything else to God . . . including your children.

Today's Prayer

Dear Lord, when I am worried,
I know where to turn for help: to those
who love me and to You. Thank You
for the people who love and care for
me, and thank You, Lord, for Your love.
Because of that love, I have hope
and assurance for this day
and every day.
Amen

God Looks On the Inside

God judges persons differently than humans do. Men and women look at the face; God looks into the heart.

1 Samuel 16:7 MSG

Other people see you from the outside, and sometimes people will judge you by the way you look. But God doesn't care how you look on the outside. Why? Because God is wiser than that; God cares about what you are on the inside—God sees your heart.

If you're like most people, you'll worry a little bit about the way you look (or maybe you'll worry a lot about it). But please don't worry too much about your appearance!

How you look on the outside isn't important . . . but how you feel on the inside is important. So don't worry about trying to impress other people. Instead of trying to impress other kids, try to impress God by being the best person you can be.

If the narrative of the Scriptures teaches us
anything, from the serpent in the Garden to
the carpenter in Nazareth, it teaches us that things
are rarely what they seem, that we shouldn't
be fooled by appearances.

John Eldredge

A Kid's Tip!

Beauty on the outside isn't important . . . beauty on
the inside is.

A Parent's Tip!

If you truly believe that beauty begins on the
inside, make sure your actions match your beliefs.
Your children don't need mixed messages.

Today's Prayer

Dear Lord, You know my heart.
Help me to say things,
to do things, and to think things
that are pleasing to You.
Amen

Day 34

Got a Question? Ask God

Continue to ask, and God will give to you.
Continue to search, and you will find.
Continue to knock, and the door
will open for you.

Matthew 7:7 ICB

Is God hanging out at the far end of the universe, too far away to hear your requests? Nope, God is right here, right now, waiting to hear from you. Are you ready to talk to Him? Hopefully, you've learned the wisdom of asking God for His help.

Are you in need? Ask God to sustain you. Are you troubled? Take your worries to Him, and He will comfort you. Are you weary? Seek God's strength. Do you have questions about your future that you simply can't answer? Ask your Heavenly Father for insight and direction. In all things great and small, seek God's wisdom and His will. He will hear your prayers, and He will answer.

God's help is always available,
but it is only given to those who seek it.

Max Lucado

A Kid's Tip!

Today, think of a specific need that is weighing heavily on your heart. Then, spend a few quiet moments asking God for His guidance and for His help.

A Parent's Tip!

Do you have questions that you simply cannot answer? If so, you are not alone. God does not always explain Himself in ways that we, as mere mortals, can easily understand. So, instead of asking, "Why me, Lord?" perhaps you should ask, "What next, Lord?" Even when you cannot find easy answers, you can still find new direction. And you should.

Today's Prayer

Dear Lord, the Bible tells me that when
I ask for Your help, You will give it.
I thank You, Lord, for Your help,
for Your love, and for Your Son.
Amen

Day 35

Choose
a Good Attitude

Your attitude should be the same
that Christ Jesus had.

Philippians 2:5 NLT

*G*od knows everything about you, including your attitude. And when your attitude is good, God is pleased . . . very pleased.

Are you interested in pleasing God? Are you interested in pleasing your parents? Your teachers? And your friends? If so, try to make your attitude the best it can be. When you try hard to have a good attitude, you'll make other people feel better—and you'll make yourself feel better, too.

We must admit that we spend more of our time concentrating and fretting over the things that can't be changed than we do giving attention to the one thing we can change: our choice of attitude.

Charles Swindoll

A Kid's Tip!

Learn about Jesus and His attitude. Then try to do what Jesus would do.

A Parent's Tip!

They can read your mind: Kids (and spouses) are amazingly sensitive. So be careful with your thoughts as well as your actions.

Today's Prayer

Dear Lord, I pray for an attitude that pleases You. Even when I'm angry, unhappy, tired, or upset, I pray that I can remember what it means to be a good person and a good Christian.
Amen

Day 36

The Blame Game

People's own foolishness ruins their lives,
but in their minds they blame the Lord.

Proverbs 19:3 NCV

When something goes wrong, do you look for somebody to blame? And do you try to blame other people even if you're the one who made the mistake? Hopefully not!

It's silly to try to blame other people for your own mistakes, so don't do it.

If you've done something you're ashamed of, don't look for somebody to blame; look for a way to say, "I'm sorry, and I won't make that same mistake again."

You'll never win the blame game,
so why even bother to play?

Marie T. Freeman

A Kid's Tip!

Blaming others is easy . . . but it's usually wrong.
Fixing mistakes is harder . . . but it's usually right.

A Parent's Tip!

Blaming others is easy, Part II . . . It's easy (and
quite natural) for your child to find fault in others
and spread blame to others. That's why it's up
to you, as a parent, to teach your child to take
responsibility . . . and to learn from his mistakes!

Today's Prayer

Dear Lord, when I make a mistake,
I want to admit it. Help me not blame
others for the mistakes that I make.
And when I make a mistake,
help me to learn from it.

Amen

Day 37

It's a Celebration

Celebrate God all day, every day.
I mean, revel in him!

Philippians 4:4 MSG

Do you feel like celebrating today? Hopefully, you do feel like celebrating! After all, today (like every other day) should be a special time to thank God for all the wonderful things He has given you.

So don't wait for birthdays or holidays—make every day a special day, including this one. Take time to pause and thank God for His gifts. And then demonstrate your thanks by celebrating His world, His blessings, and His love.

The Christian lifestyle is not one of
legalistic do's and don'ts,
but one that is positive,
attractive, and joyful.

Vonette Bright

A Parent's Tip and a Kid's Tip!

If you don't feel like celebrating, start counting
your blessings. Before long, you'll realize that you
have plenty of reasons to celebrate.

Today's Prayer

Dear Lord, help me remember that every day is cause for celebration. Today I will try my best to keep joy in my heart. I will celebrate the life You have given me here on earth and the eternal life that will be mine in heaven.

Amen

Day 38

Bless Others

If you have two shirts, share with
the person who does not have one.
If you have food, share that too.

Luke 3:11 ICB

Lots of people in the world aren't as fortunate as you are. Some of these folks live in faraway places, and that makes it harder to help them. But other people who need your help are living very near you.

Ask your parents to help you find ways to do something nice for folks who need it. And don't forget that everybody needs love, kindness, and respect, so you should always be ready to share those things, too.

The Lord has abundantly blessed me all of my life.
I'm not trying to pay Him back for all
of His wonderful gifts; I just realize that
He gave them to me to give away.

Lisa Whelchel

A Kid's Tip!

Too many toys? Give them away! Are you one of
those lucky kids who has more toys than you can
play with? If so, remember that not everyone is
so lucky. Ask your parents to help you give some
of your toys to children who need them more than
you do.

A Parent's Tip!

Kids will follow your lead. Don't forget to go through
your toys, too.

Today's Prayer

Dear Lord, I know there is no happiness
in keeping Your blessings for myself.
Today, I will share my blessings with
my family, with my friends,
and people who need my help.
Amen

Day 39

Smiling Is Good

Jacob said, "For what a relief it is
to see your friendly smile.
It is like seeing the smile of God!"

Genesis 33:10 NLT

The Bible tells us that a cheerful heart is like medicine: it makes us feel better. Where does cheerfulness begin? It begins inside each of us; it begins in the heart. So let's be thankful to God for His blessings, and let's show our thanks by sharing good cheer wherever we go.

Today, make sure that you share a smile and a kind word with as many people as you can. This old world needs all the cheering up it can get . . . and so do your friends.

Life goes on. Keep on smiling
and the whole world smiles with you.

Dennis Swanberg

A Kid's Tip!

Smile as much as you can. It's good for your health,
and it makes those around you feel better.

A Parent's Tip!

If you'd like to see a big smile on your child's face,
start by putting a big smile on yours.

Today's Prayer

Dear Lord, put a smile on my face,
and let me share that smile
with my friends and family.
Amen

Day 40

Choose Kindness

The thing you should want most is
God's kingdom and doing what God wants.
Then all these other things you need
will be given to you.

Matthew 6:33 NCV

There's really no way to get around it: choices matter. If you make good choices, good things will usually happen to you. And if you make bad choices, bad things will usually happen.

The next time you have an important choice to make, ask yourself this: "Am I doing what God wants me to do?" If you can answer that question with a great big "YES," then go ahead. But if you're not sure if the choice you are about to make is right, slow down. Why? Because choices matter . . . a lot!

God is voting for us all the time.
The devil is voting against us all the time.
The way we vote carries the election.

Corrie ten Boom

A Kid's Tip!

When you make wise choices . . . you make everybody happy. You make your parents happy, you make your teachers happy, you make your friends happy, and you make God happy!

A Parent's Tip!

Some choices are up to the parents: Certainly, we want to give our children the chance to make decisions on their own, but some decisions must be reserved for the wisest men and women of the family (responsible parents like you). When it comes to the health, well-being, and safety of your child, you must decide.

Today's Prayer

Dear God, I have many choices to make.
Help me choose wisely as I follow in
the footsteps of Your Son Jesus.
Amen

Day 41

Jesus Loves Me

I have loved you even as the Father
has loved me. Remain in my love.

John 15:9 NLT

Y ou've probably heard the song "Jesus Loves Me." And exactly how much does He love you? He loves you so much that He gave His life so that you might live forever with Him in heaven.

How can you repay Christ's love? By accepting Him into your heart and by obeying His rules. When you do, He will love you and bless you today, tomorrow, and forever.

Jesus: the proof of God's love.

Philip Yancey

A Kid's Tip!

What a friend you have in Jesus: Jesus loves you, and He offers you eternal life with Him in heaven. Welcome Him into your heart. Now!

A Parent's Tip!

Jesus loves you. His love can—and should—be the cornerstone and the touchstone of your life.

Today's Prayer

Dear Jesus, I know that You love me
today and that You will love me forever.
And I thank You for Your love . . .
today and forever.
Amen

Day 42

Church Is a Kind Place

Don't you realize that all of you together
are the temple of God and that
the Spirit of God lives in you?

1 Corinthians 3:16 NLT

When your parents take you to church, are you pleased to go? Hopefully so. After all, church is a wonderful place to learn about God's rules.

The church belongs to God just as surely as you belong to God. That's why the church is a good place to learn about God and about His Son Jesus.

So when your mom and dad take you to church, remember this: church is a fine place to be . . . and you're lucky to be there.

The church needs people who are doers
of the Word and not just hearers.

Warren Wiersbe

A Kid's Tip!

Forget the excuses: If somebody starts making up
reasons not to go to church, don't pay any attention
. . . even if that person is you!

A Parent's Tip!

Make it a celebration, not an obligation: Your
attitude toward church will help determine your
kid's attitude toward church . . . so celebrate
accordingly!

Today's Prayer

Dear Lord, thank You for my church.
When I am at church, I will be generous,
kind, well-behaved, and respectful.
And when I am not at church,
I will act the same way.

Amen

Day 43

Feeling Better

Believe me, I do my level best to keep
a clear conscience before God and
my neighbors in everything I do.

Acts 24:16 MSG

When you know that you're doing what's right, you'll feel better about yourself. Why? Because you have a little voice in your head called your "conscience." Your conscience is a feeling that tells you whether something is right or wrong—and it's a feeling that makes you feel better about yourself when you know you've done the right thing.

Your conscience is an important tool. Pay attention to it!

The more you listen to your conscience, the easier it is to behave yourself. So here's great advice: first, slow down long enough to figure out the right thing to do—and then do it! When you do, you'll be proud of yourself . . . and other people will be proud of you, too.

My conscience is captive to the word of God.

Martin Luther

A Kid's Tip!

If you're not sure what to do . . . trust your conscience. It's the little voice that tells you right from wrong; listen to it and believe it. It's almost always right!

A Parent's Tip!

Sometimes, the little voice that we hear in our heads can be the echoes of our own parents' voices . . . and now that we're parents ourselves, we're the ones whose words will echo down through the hearts and minds of future generations. It's a big responsibility, but with God's help, we're up to the challenge.

Today's Prayer

Dear Lord, You have given me a conscience that tells me what is right and what is wrong. I will listen to that quiet voice so I can do the right thing today and every day.

Amen

Day 44

The Gift of Contentment

I've learned by now to be quite content whatever my circumstances. I'm just as happy with little as with much, with much as with little. I've found the recipe for being happy whether full or hungry, hands full or hands empty.

Philippians 4:11-12 MSG

Where can we find contentment? Is it a result of being wealthy or famous? Nope. Genuine contentment is a gift from God to those who trust Him and follow His commandments.

If we don't find contentment in God, we will never find it anywhere else. But, if we seek Him and obey Him, we will be blessed with joyful, peaceful, meaningful lives. When God dwells at the center of our lives, peace and contentment will belong to us just as surely as we belong to God.

When we do what is right, we have contentment,
peace, and happiness.

Beverly LaHaye

A Kid's Tip!

If you want to be contented . . . you should obey the
rules you find in God's Word, you should obey your
parents, and you should learn to trust that quiet
voice that tells you right from wrong (that voice is
called your conscience, and you should listen to it
very carefully).

A Parent's Tip!

Contentment comes, not from your circumstances
or your possessions, but from your attitude. And
remember this: peace with God is the foundation of
a contented life and a contented family.

Today's Prayer

Dear Lord, when I welcome Jesus into
my heart, and when I obey
Your commandments, I will be contented.
Help me to trust Your Word and follow
Your Son today and forever.
Amen

Day 45

The Fun of Cooperating

Two people can accomplish more than
twice as much as one;
they get a better return for their labor.

Ecclesiastes 4:9 NLT

Helping other people can be fun! When you help others, you feel better about yourself. And, you know that God approves of what you're doing.

When you learn how to cooperate with your family and friends, you'll soon discover that it's more fun when everybody works together. And one way that you can all work together is by sharing.

So do yourself a favor: learn better ways to share and to cooperate. It's the right thing to do, and besides: it's more fun.

Teamwork makes the dream work.

John Maxwell

A Kid's Tip!

Cooperation pays. When you cooperate with your friends and family, you'll feel good about yourself— and your family and friends will feel good about you, too.

A Parent's Tip!

Teaching cooperation: You know that your children can accomplish much more in life by working cooperatively with others. So it's up to you to teach the fine art of cooperation. And make no mistake: the best way to teach the art of cooperation is by example.

Today's Prayer

Dear Lord, help me learn to be kind,
courteous, and cooperative
with my family and with my friends.
Amen

Day 46

Heaven

Be glad and rejoice,
because your reward is great in heaven.

Matthew 5:12 Holman CSB

It's time to remind yourself of a promise that God made a long time ago—the promise that God sent His Son Jesus to save the world and to save you! And when you stop to think about it, there can be no greater promise than that.

No matter where you are, God is with you. God loves you, and He sent His Son so that you can live forever in heaven with your loved ones. WOW! That's the greatest promise in the history of the universe. The End.

God's people have always tied their lives
to a single hope, the assurance of one day
seeing God in heaven.

Warren Wiersbe

A Kid's Tip!

Heaven is all those wonderful things you wish you
had on earth . . . and so very much more.

A Parent's Tip!

God has created heaven and given you a way to
get there. The rest is up to you. Make sure your
children know the way.

Today's Prayer

Dear Lord, I thank You for the gift
of eternal life that is mine through
Your Son Jesus. I will keep the promise
of heaven in my heart
today and every day.
Amen

Set the Example

You are young, but do not let anyone
treat you as if you were not important.
Be an example to show the believers
how they should live. Show them
with your words, with the way you live,
with your love, with your faith,
and with your pure life.

1 Timothy 4:12 ICB

What kind of example are you? Are you the kind of person who shows other people what it means to be kind and forgiving? Hopefully so!!!

How hard is it to say a kind word? Not very! How hard is it to accept someone's apology? Usually not too hard. So today, be a good example for others to follow. Because God needs people, like you, who are willing to stand up and be counted for Him. And that's exactly the kind of example you should try to be.

Living life with a consistent spiritual walk deeply
influences those we love most.

Vonette Bright

A Kid's Tip!

Your friends are watching: so be the kind of
example that God wants you to be—be a good
example.

A Parent's Tip!

Calling all parents! What the world needs is more
parents who are willing to be positive role models
to their children. God wants you to be that kind of
parent . . . now!

Today's Prayer

Lord, make me a good example to
my family and friends. Let the things
that I say and do show everybody
what it means to be a good person
and a good Christian.

Amen

Day 48

Saying Your Sorry

Make this your common practice:
Confess your sins to each other and
pray for each other so that you can live
together whole and healed. The prayer
of a person living right with God is
something powerful to be reckoned with.

James 5:16 MSG

When you make a mistake or hurt someone's feelings, what should you do? You should say you're sorry and ask for forgiveness. And you should do so sooner, not later.

The longer you wait to apologize, the harder it is on you. So if you've done something wrong, don't be afraid to ask for forgiveness, and don't be afraid to ask for it NOW!

The more you practice the art of forgiving,
the quicker you'll master the art of living.

Marie T. Freeman

A Kid's Tip!

When you make mistakes, are you genuinely sorry?
If so, be sure that you apologize and make things
right.

A Parent's Tip!

It is not a sign of weakness when you apologize to
your child. If you make a mistake, say so. When you
do, your child will learn an invaluable lesson.

Today's Prayer

Dear Lord, whenever I make a mistake,
let me be wise enough to say I am sorry.
And let me learn the lessons I need
to learn, today and every day.
Amen

Day 49

God First

Jesus answered, "'Love the Lord your
God with all your heart, all your soul,
and all your mind.' This is the first
and most important command."

Matthew 22:37-38 NCV

Are you willing to put God first, or do you put other things ahead of your love for Him? God wants you to love Him first, and He wants you to obey Him first. When you do these things, you'll be happy you did!

When the Pharisees quizzed Jesus about God's most important commandment, Jesus answered, "Love the Lord your God with all your heart, all your soul, and all your mind. This is the first and most important command" (Matthew 22:37-38 NCV). So if you want to do the right thing, always put Him in the place He deserves: first place.

God can see clearly no matter how dark
or foggy the night is.
Trust His Word to guide you safely home.

Lisa Whelchel

A Kid's Tip!

Talk to your parents about some of the ways you can
put God in first place.

A Parent's Tip!

Is He first in your family? Every family puts
something or someone in first place. Does
God occupy first place in your family? If so,
congratulations! If not, it's time to reorder your
priorities.

Today's Prayer

Dear Lord, it's easy to talk about putting You first, but it's harder to do it in real life. Please help me put You first—really first—and not just talk about it.
Amen

Day 50

God Is Love

Whoever does not love
does not know God,
because God is love.

1 John 4:8 ICB

The Bible tells us that God is love and that if we wish to know Him we must have love in our hearts. Sometimes, of course, when we're tired, frustrated, or angry, it is very hard for us to be loving. Thankfully, anger and frustration are feelings that come and go, but God's love lasts forever.

If you'd like to improve your day and your life, share God's love with your family and friends. Every time you love, every time you are kind, and every time you give, God smiles.

If God had a refrigerator, your picture would be
on it. If he had a wallet, your photo would be in it.
He sends you flowers every spring
and a sunrise every morning.

Max Lucado

A Kid's Tip!

Show and tell: It's good to tell your loved ones how
you feel about them, but that's not enough. You
should also show them how you feel with your good
deeds and your kind words.

A Parent's Tip!

You know that "God is love." Now, it's your
responsibility to make certain that your children
know it, too.

Today's Prayer

Dear Lord, make me a person who is
loving and giving. You first loved me,
Father. Let me, in turn, love others,
and let my behavior show them that
I love them, today and forever.
Amen